ACCA

Audit and assurance (AA)

Pocket Notes

British library cataloguing-in-publication data

A catalogue record for this book is available from the British Library.

Published by:
Kaplan Publishing UK
Unit 2 The Business Centre
Molly Millars Lane
Wokingham
Berkshire
RG41 2QZ

ISBN: 978-1-78740-916-3

Printed and bound in Great Britain.

Acknowledgements

This Product includes propriety content of the International Accounting Standards Board which is overseen by the IFRS Foundation, and is used with the express permission of the IFRS Foundation under licence. All rights reserved. No part of this publication may be reproduced, stored in a retrieval system, or transmitted in any form or by any means, electronic, mechanical, photocopying, recording, or otherwise, without prior written permission of Kaplan Publishing and the IFRS Foundation.

The IFRS Foundation logo, the IASB logo, the IFRS for SMEs logo, the "Hexagon Device", "IFRS Foundation", "eIFRS", "IAS", "IASB", "IFRS for SMEs", "IFRS", "IASs", "IFRSs", "International Accounting Standards" and "International Financial Reporting Standards", "IFRIC" and "IFRS Taxonomy" are Trade Marks of the IFRS Foundation.

Trade Marks

The IFRS Foundation logo, the IASB logo, the IFRS for SMEs logo, the "Hexagon Device", "IFRS Foundation", "eIFRS", "IAS", "IASB", "IFRS for SMEs", "NIIF" IASs" "IFRS", "IFRSs", "International Accounting Standards", "International Financial Reporting Standards", "IFRIC", "SIC" and "IFRS Taxonomy".

Further details of the Trade Marks including details of countries where the Trade Marks are registered or applied for are available from the Foundation on request.

This product contains material that is ©Financial Reporting Council Ltd (FRC). Adapted and reproduced with the kind permission of the Financial Reporting Council. All rights reserved. For further information, please visit www.frc.org.uk or call +44 (0)20 7492 2300.

Contents

This document references IFRS® Standards and IAS® Standards, which are authored by the International Accounting Standards Board (the Board), and published in the 2019 IFRS Standards Red Book.

Exam format

		Number of marks
Section A:	3 x 10 mark objective test case study questions	30
Section B:	1 x 30 mark question	30
	2 x 20 mark questions	40
		100

Time allowed: 3 hours

Aim of the paper

To develop knowledge and understanding of the process of carrying out the assurance engagement and its application in the context of the professional regulatory framework.

Keys to success

Answer the question

Read the question extremely carefully, paying attention to the verbs telling you what to do, and to the mark allocation. You must make (at least) one point in your answer for every mark available.

Don't overrun your time allocation

You must be absolutely strict with yourself with your time allocation for each question. In the exam room, write down the times for each question, and force yourself to finish your attempt within the time available. Such discipline may not be fun, but it is the approach that will earn you most marks in the exam.

Think before you start writing

Take time to understand what the question is **really** asking. Certain words read in isolation may lead you to misinterpret the requirement.

You also need to make sure that you identify the whole requirement. Some questions are actually more than one requirement. For example:

"Identify and explain the control deficiencies in the question **and** recommend solutions to overcome them."

Quality and accuracy are of the utmost importance to us so if you spot an error in any of our products, please send an email to mykaplanreporting@kaplan.com with full details, or follow the link to the feedback form in MyKaplan.

Our Quality Co-ordinator will work with our technical team to verify the error and take action to ensure it is corrected in future editions.

chapter

1

Introduction to assurance

In this chapter

- Elements of an assurance engagement.
- Reasonable and limited assurance.
- Accountability, stewardship and agency.
- Benefits and limitations of audit.

Elements of an assurance engagement

Purpose of assurance is to increase the confidence of the user in the subject matter being relied upon

3 Party Involvement	• **Practitioner** e.g. auditor (performs an independent examination of the subject matter against the suitable criteria and provides a written assurance report) • **Intended user** e.g. shareholders (user of the subject matter) • **Responsible party** e.g. directors (preparer of the subject matter)
Subject Matter	The information being examined e.g. financial statements
Suitable Criteria	Subject matter is judged against the criteria e.g. IFRS
Evidence	Sufficient and appropriate to provide a basis for the conclusion
Written Assurance Report	Expressing a conclusion or opinion

Reasonable and limited assurance

The Framework permits only two types of assurance engagement to be performed:

Reasonable assurance engagements

The practitioner:

- Gathers sufficient appropriate evidence
- Does enough work to be able to draw reasonable, but not absolute, conclusions
- Concludes that the subject matter conforms in all material respects with identified suitable criteria
- Gives a report in the form of **a positive statement of opinion**

EXAMPLE

- Statutory audit.

Limited assurance engagement

The practitioner:

- Gathers sufficient appropriate evidence to be satisfied that the subject matter is plausible in the circumstances
- Gives a report in the form of **a negative statement of conclusion** ("nothing has come to our attention")

EXAMPLES

- Review of financial statements (International Standard on Review Engagements 2400).
- Risk assessment reports.
- Performance measurement reports.
- Systems reliability reports.
- Reports on social and environmental issues reviews of internal control.

Accountability, stewardship and agency

Accountability

People in positions of power can be held to account for their actions

Directors are accountable to the shareholders for the decisions they make in relation to the company

Stewardship

The responsibility to take good care of resources. Known as a 'fiduciary relationship'

Directors are the stewards of the company

Directors are required to produce financial statements giving an account of their stewardship

Agency

When one party, the principal, employs another party, the agent, to perform a task of their behalf

Directors are the agents of the shareholders

External auditors are the agents of the shareholders

Company management are required to produce financial statements giving an account of their stewardship of the company at regular intervals, but there was a need for some kind of independent validation of the financial statements – the independent audit.

Benefits and limitations of audit

Benefits of audit

- Helps improve quality of information.
- Independent scrutiny.
- Reduces risk of management bias, fraud and error.
- Enhances credibility of FS.
- Deficiencies in internal controls highlighted.

Limitations of audit

- FS include subjective estimates and judgments.
- Inherent limitations of internal controls.
- Representations from management not reliable.
- Evidence is persuasive not conclusive.
- Do not test all transactions, only a sample.

Expectations Gap

- Auditor tests everything.
- Auditor detects all fraud and error.
- Auditor confirms the company is a going concern.
- Auditor prepares the FS.

Exam focus

To practise the basics use the following test your understandings (TYUs) Study Text:

- Chapter 1, TYU 1
- Chapter 1, TYU 2
- Chapter 1, TYU 3

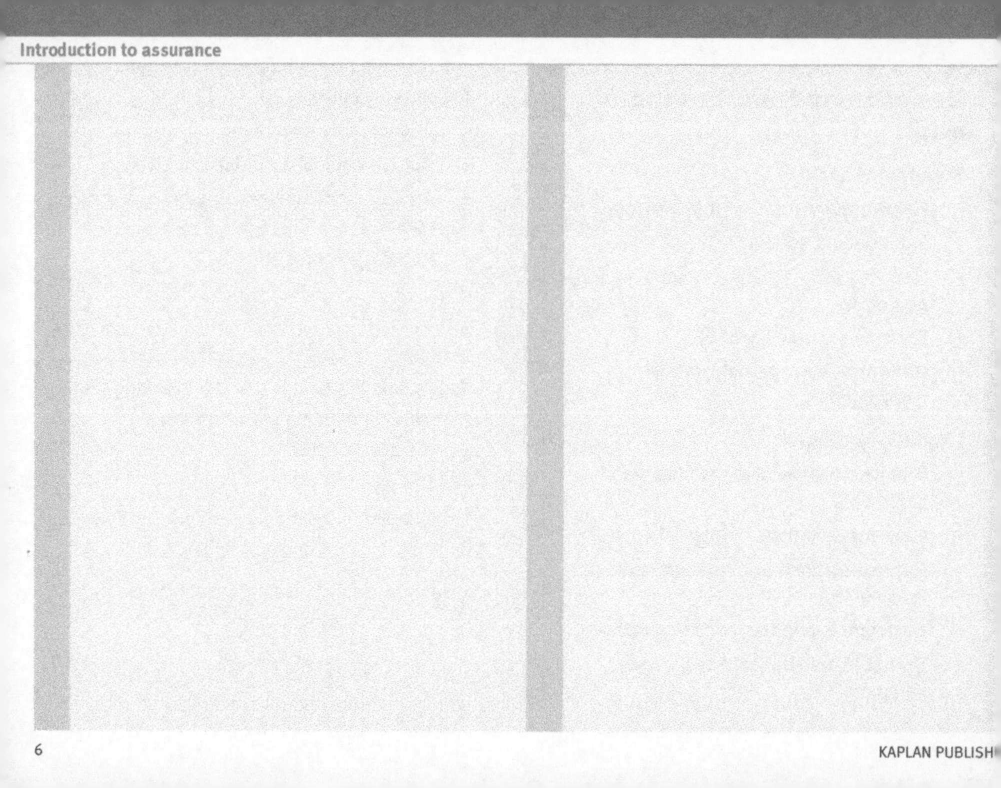

chapter

2

Rules and regulation

In this chapter

- International and UK standard setting and regulation.
- Why have an audit.
- Who may or may not act as an auditor.
- How are auditors appointed and removed.
- Auditor's rights and duties.

International and UK standard setting and regulation

IFAC

International Federation of Accountants

A grouping of accountancy bodies (including ACCA)

No legal standing in members countries

IAASB

International Audit and Assurance Standards Board

A subsidiary of IFAC

Sets international standards on auditing (ISAs)

In the EU all audits must be carried out in accordance with ISAs for accounting periods beginning on or after 1 January 2005

- ISAs are adopted, and modified if necessary, by individual countries or they can set their own standards.
- Any modifications reflect the legislation relating to companies in the country that the client is based, which may be different from that in other jurisdictions.
- Local law overrides ISAs.

Why have an audit

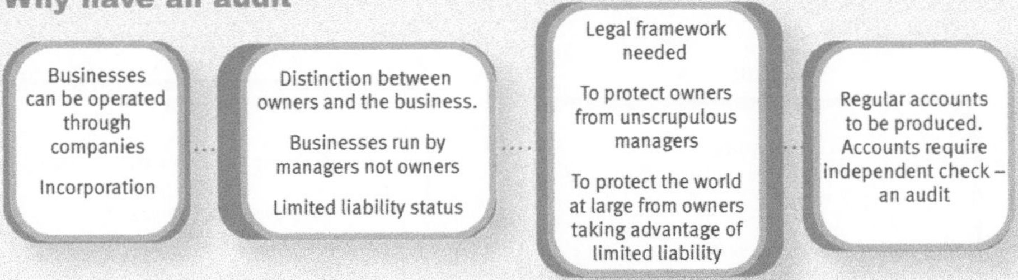

Businesses can be operated through companies

Incorporation

Distinction between owners and the business.

Businesses run by managers not owners

Limited liability status

Legal framework needed

To protect owners from unscrupulous managers

To protect the world at large from owners taking advantage of limited liability

Regular accounts to be produced. Accounts require independent check – an audit

- Therefore in most countries companies require an audit.
- In many countries there is an exemption for small businesses.

Who may or may not act as an auditor

MAY ACT ✓

INDIVIDUALS

- A member of a Recognised Supervisory Body (RSB) e.g. ACCA
  and
- Allowed by the rules of that body to be an auditor
  or
- Someone directly authorised by the state.

FIRMS

- Controlled by members of a suitably authorised supervisory body
  Or
- A firm directly authorised by the state.

MAY NOT ACT ✗

EXCLUDED BY LAW

In Britain

- An officer (Director or secretary) of the company
  - an employee of the company
  - a business partner or employee of the above.

EXCLUDED BY ETHICS

- Due to lack of objectivity or independence, for example, due to:
  - close business relationships
  - personal relationships
  - long association with the client
  - fee dependency
  - non-audit services provided.

How are auditors appointed and removed

APPOINTMENT

In most jurisdictions

- The members (shareholders) of the company.
- Directors can appoint first auditor and fill a 'casual vacancy', but needs members' approval at next AGM.
- Appointment runs from end of AGM until the end of the next AGM.
- Where no AGM – automatic annual reappointment unless a shareholder objects.

REMOVAL

- Simple majority at a general meeting of the company.
- The law requires special notice to be given.
- Resignation (auditors may have to submit to members a statement of the circumstances surrounding their resignation).

Auditor's rights and duties

Rights

- Access at all times to all books and records
- Receive information and explanations from the officers of the company
- Receive notice of and attend company meetings
- Speak at such meetings
- Receive copies of any written resolutions of the company
- Requisition an Extraordinary General Meeting (EGM) on resignation
- Require notice of circumstances relating to resignation to be circulated.

Duties

- Report to the members on whether the financial statements give a true and fair view and have been properly prepared.

Exam focus

To practise the basics use the following test your understandings (TYUs) from the Study Text:

- TYU 1
- TYU 2

chapter

3

Corporate governance

In this chapter

- Corporate governance.
- Audit committees.

Corporate governance

Corporate governance is about ensuring that companies are run well in the interests of their shareholders and the wider community. Need arose due to high profile collapses of companies.

Good corporate governance is particularly important for publicly traded companies.

Maintaining satisfactory standards of corporate governance is the responsibility of those operating a company.

The board

The key responsibilities of the board are:

- Reviewing and guiding corporate strategy
- Monitoring the effectiveness of the company's governance practices and making changes as needed
- Selecting, compensating, monitoring and, when necessary, replacing key executives
- Aligning key executive and board remuneration
- Monitoring and managing potential conflicts of interest of management, board members and shareholders
- Ensuring the integrity of the corporation's accounting and financial reporting systems, overseeing the process of disclosure and communications.

Note the term "Board" primarily to mean the Supervisory board in a 2 tier board arrangement or the non-executive directors and relevant sub committees in a unitary board structure.

Corporate governance in action

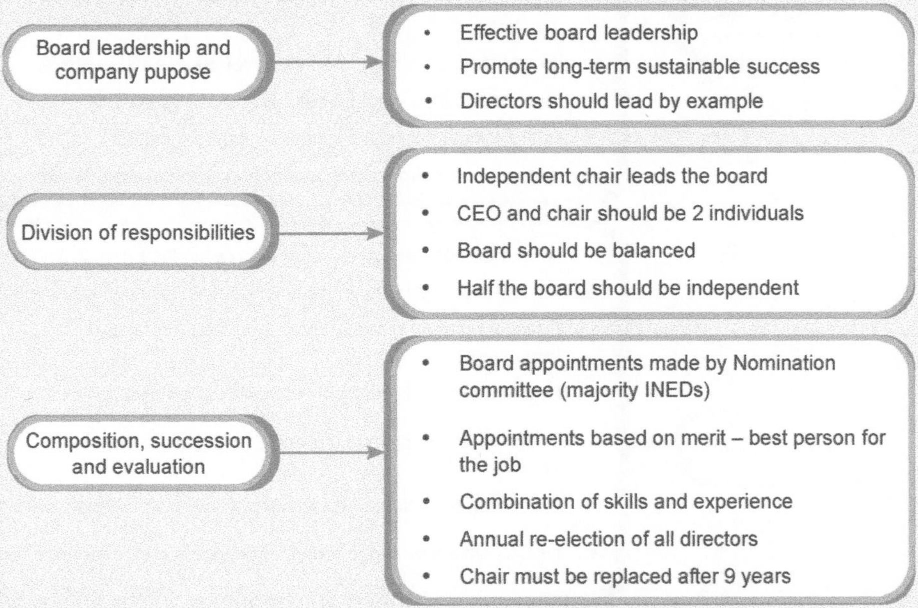

Board leadership and company pupose

- Effective board leadership
- Promote long-term sustainable success
- Directors should lead by example

Division of responsibilities

- Independent chair leads the board
- CEO and chair should be 2 individuals
- Board should be balanced
- Half the board should be independent

Composition, succession and evaluation

- Board appointments made by Nomination committee (majority INEDs)
- Appointments based on merit – best person for the job
- Combination of skills and experience
- Annual re-election of all directors
- Chair must be replaced after 9 years

Audit, risk and internal control

- Audit committee should ensure independence of IA and EA functions
- Board should manage risks and oversee internal controls
- Audit committee must be established (min 3 INEDs)
- Chair should not be a member of audit committee
- At least one member with recent and relevant experience

Remuneration

- Remuneration set by Remuneration committee (min 3 INEDs)
- Remuneration should promote long-term sustainable success
- Policy for setting remuneration should be formal and transparent
- No director should be involved in setting his own pay
- Board chair can only be a member of RC if independent on appointment
- Workforce pay should be considered when setting exec pay
- NEDs paid according to time commitments and responsibilities

Audit committees

Composition

- 3 independent non-executives.
- At least 1 with financial expertise.

Objectives

- Public confidence in the credibility and objectivity of published financial information.
- Assisting directors in meeting their responsibilities in respect of financial reporting.
- Liaison with external auditors.

Function

- Monitoring integrity of the financial statements.
- Reviewing internal financial controls.
- Monitoring and reviewing internal audit function.
- Making recommendations re appointment, removal and remuneration of the external auditor.
- Reviewing and monitoring the external auditor's independence and objectivity and the effectiveness of the audit process.
- Developing and implementing policy on the engagement of the external auditor to supply non-audit services.
- Reviewing arrangements for confidential reporting by employees and investigation of possible improprieties – whistle blowing.

The audit committee and internal audit

The audit committee should:

- Ensure internal auditor has direct access to the board chair and to the audit committee.
- Review and assess the annual internal audit work plan.
- Receive reports on the results of internal audit work.
- If no IA function in place, review need for one annually.

Risk management

All companies face risks of many kinds.

Companies must address the risk issues and:

- Identify the risks faced (e.g. operational, financial, legal)
- May maintain a risk register
- Assess the relative importance of each risk
- Sometimes accept the risk as an inevitable part of its operations.

Exam focus

Exam kit questions in this area:

Section A – Objective test case questions:

- Sistar
- Cameron
- Kingfisher

Section B – Constructed response questions

- Freesia
- Saxophone Enterprises

chapter

4

Ethics and acceptance

In this chapter

- ACCA code of ethics and conduct.
- Independence and objectivity.
- Fundamental principles, threats and safeguards.
- Fundamental principles.
- Threats and safeguards.
- Confidentiality.
- Acceptance of engagements.
- New work and the engagement letter.

ACCA code of ethics and conduct

- The **user** needs to believe that assurance practitioners act in accordance with a code of ethics, and
- The **practitioner** needs a code of ethics to make sure that he or she is worthy of that level of trust.

SOURCES

ACCA Code of Ethics and Conduct

IESBA International Code for Professional Accountants

Similar conceptual frameworks

CONTENTS

Fundamental principles of ethical behaviour

Potential threats to ethical behaviour

Possible safeguards which can be implemented to counter the threats

Remember:

- The Codes of Ethics provide guidance that the auditor must follow.
- In some cases the only viable safeguard is not to accept an assurance engagement, or to resign from it.
- The ACCA reserves the right to discipline members who infringe the rules through a process of disciplinary hearings.

Independence and objectivity

- Independence is freedom from any external control or influence in making decisions.
- Objectivity is the state of mind which has regard to all considerations relevant to the task in hand but no other.

Fundamental principles, threats and safeguards

FUNDAMENTAL PRINCIPLES
- Integrity
- Objectivity
- Professional competence and due care
- Confidentiality
- Professional behaviour

THREATS
- Self-interest
- Self-review
- Advocacy
- Familiarity
- Intimidation

SAFEGUARDS
- Segregation of duties
- Review
- Rotation
- Ceasing to act
- Separate teams
- Engagement quality review

Fundamental principles

The code identifies five fundamental principles in professional conduct.

- **Integrity:** Members should be straightforward and honest in all professional and business relationships.
- **Objectivity:** Members should not allow bias, conflicts of interest or undue influence of others to override professional or business judgements.
- **Professional competence and due care:** A professional accountant must attain and maintain professional knowledge and skill at the level required to ensure that a client or employer receives a competent and professional service.
- **Confidentiality:** Members should respect the confidentiality of information acquired as a result of professional and business relationships and should not disclose any such information to third parties without proper and specific authority or unless there is a legal or professional right or duty to disclose.
- **Professional behaviour:** Members should comply with relevant laws and regulations and should avoid any action that discredits the profession.

Threats and safeguards

Members are required to apply the conceptual framework to identify threats to compliance with the fundamental principles, to evaluate their significance and, if such threats are other than clearly insignificant, to apply safeguards to eliminate them or reduce them to an acceptable level such that compliance with the fundamental principles is not compromised.

Example Threat	Possible safeguard
Auditor owns shares in the client (Self-interest)	Sell the shares as soon as possible.
Auditor is unduly dependent on client for fees (Self-interest)	Fees from listed clients should not exceed 15% of the total practice income for 2 consecutive years.
Significant outstanding fees due from the client (Self-interest)	Don't commence audit work until outstanding fees are paid.
Client requests contingent fee (Self-interest)	Refuse. Contingent fees are not acceptable for assurance engagements.
Gifts or hospitality from the client (Self-interest and familiarity)	Do not accept unless clearly trivial. Audit partner must authorise acceptance.
Audit partner has been in post for many years (Familiarity)	Partner rotation after 7 years for listed clients. May be extended for 1 year if audit committee approves.
Ex-auditor now works for audit client (Familiarity)	Review composition of audit team and perform EQCR.
Close relationships between auditor and client staff (Familiarity)	Remove that person from the audit team.
Auditor provides other services (Self-review)	Separate teams for each service provided. Don't provide other services to audit clients where significant reliance will be placed on the non-audit work.
Auditor is ex employee of the client (Self-review)	Don't assign that person to the audit team.
Client asks auditor to represent them in court (Advocacy)	Decline. No sufficient safeguard exists.

Confidentiality

Before disclosing, consider:

- Whether harm could be caused by the disclosure
- Whether all relevant information is knownand substantiated
- Whether the information is to be communicated to appropriate recipients

Required by law

- Production of documents or other provision of evidence in the course of legal proceedings
- To the appropriate public authorities of infringements of the law identified
- E.g. tax evasion, money laundering

Disclosure permitted by law and authorised by the client or employer

Professional duty or right to disclose, when not prohibited by law

- To comply with the quality review of ACCA or another professional body
- To respond to an inquiry or investigation by ACCA or a regulatory body
- To protect the professional interests of a professional accountant in legal proceedings
- To comply with technical standards and ethics requirements

Conflicts of Interest:

Where conflicts of interest exist, the firm's work should be arranged to avoid the interests of one being adversely affected by those of another and to prevent a breach of confidentiality.

The firm must notify all affected clients of the conflict and obtain their consent to act. The following additional safeguards should be considered:

- Advise the clients to seek independent advice
- Separate engagement teams (with different engagement partners and team members)
- Procedures to prevent access to information, e.g. physical separation of the team members and confidential/ secure data filing
- Signed confidentiality agreements
- Regular review of the application of safeguards by an independent person of appropriate seniority.

If adequate safeguards cannot be implemented, the firm must decline, or resign from one or more conflicting engagements.

Acceptance of engagements

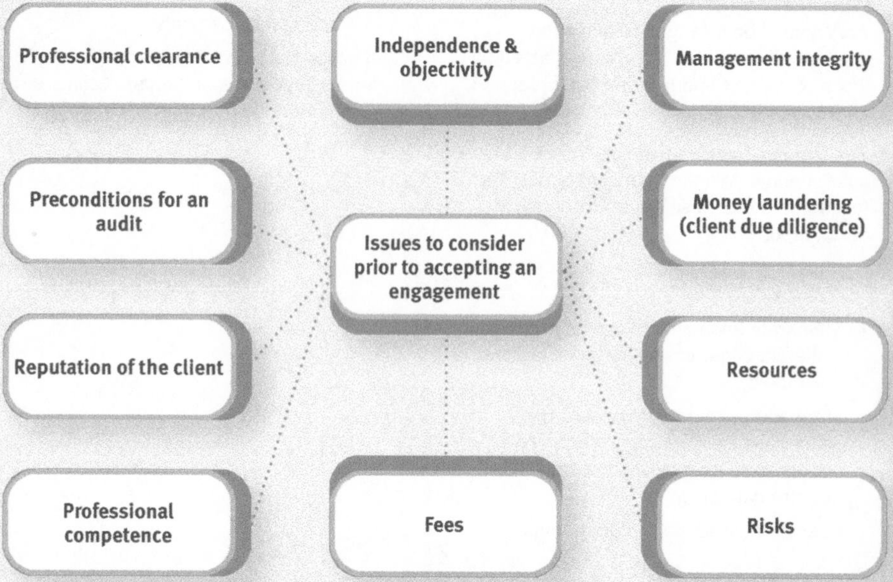

Issues to consider prior to accepting an engagement

- Professional clearance
- Independence & objectivity
- Management integrity
- Preconditions for an audit
- Money laundering (client due diligence)
- Reputation of the client
- Resources
- Professional competence
- Fees
- Risks

New work and the engagement letter

The engagement letter includes

- Responsibilities
- Objective and scope of audit
- Reference to legislation and standards
- Reference to inherent limitations of the audit
- What communications will take place
- Specific planning issues, e.g.:
  - use of internal audit
  - deadlines
  - use of experts etc
- Basis for fees

- A new letter may be sent every year to emphasise its importance to clients.
- A new letter must be sent if there have been changes, such as changes to:
  - Statutory duties
  - Professional duties
  - Other services.

Preconditions for an audit

- Acceptable financial reporting framework in place.
- Management understands its responsibility for the financial statements.
- Management understands its responsibility for internal controls.
- Management will provide the auditor with access to all information required for the audit.

Exam focus

Exam kit questions in this area:

Section A – Objective test case questions:

- Bark & Co
- Miranda & Co
- Tigger & Co
- Fir & Co
- Horti & Co
- LV Fones Co

Section B – Constructed response questions:

- Hart
- Scarlet
- Hurling
- Centipede
- Comet Publishing
- Orange Financials

chapter

5

Risk

In this chapter

- Audit risk.
- Materiality.
- Significance of the risk approach.
- Understanding the entity and its environment.
- Risk assessment procedures.
- Analytical procedures.

Audit risk

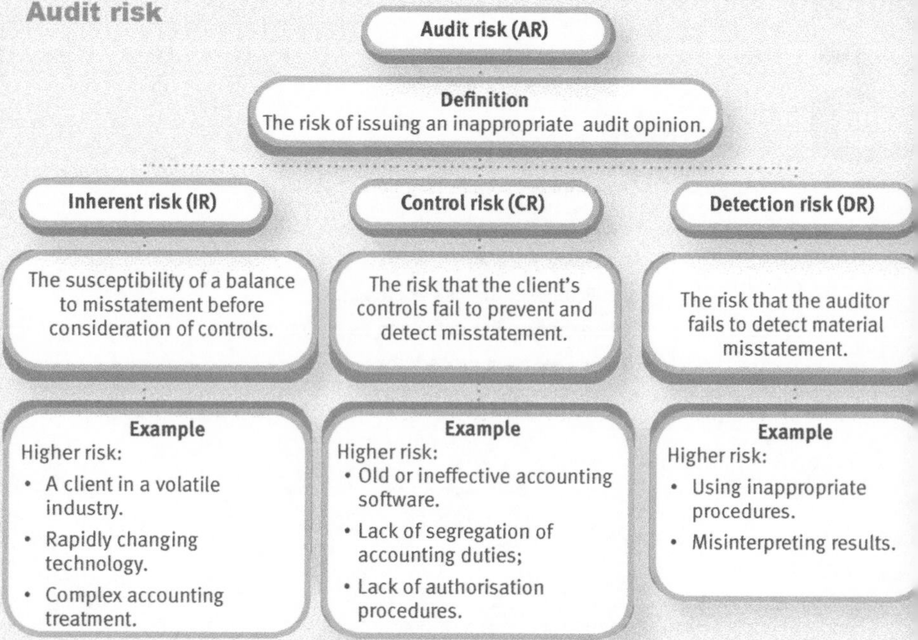

Audit risk (AR)

Definition
The risk of issuing an inappropriate audit opinion.

Inherent risk (IR)

The susceptibility of a balance to misstatement before consideration of controls.

Example
Higher risk:
- A client in a volatile industry.
- Rapidly changing technology.
- Complex accounting treatment.

Control risk (CR)

The risk that the client's controls fail to prevent and detect misstatement.

Example
Higher risk:
- Old or ineffective accounting software.
- Lack of segregation of accounting duties;
- Lack of authorisation procedures.

Detection risk (DR)

The risk that the auditor fails to detect material misstatement.

Example
Higher risk:
- Using inappropriate procedures.
- Misinterpreting results.

Materiality

Significance
Financial statements which are materially misstated will not give a true and fair view. Auditors must test all material balances

MATERIALITY

Materiality
Information is material if its omission or misstatement could, either individually or in aggregate, influence the economic decisions of users taken on the basis of the financial statements.

Determining materiality
- Size
- Nature

Performance materiality
An amount set at less than materiality for the financial statements as a whole, to reduce the risk that the aggregate of smaller misstatements in individual account balances or classes of transactions could exceed materiality for the financial statements as a whole.

- Assessing materiality is a matter of professional judgement and is not a mechanical exercise.
- Each company must be considered with reference to its unique circumstances and the informational needs of the users of the financial statements.
- In the exam, balances will be material if they exceed:
  - ½% revenue
  - 5% profit before tax
  - 1% total assets.
- Materiality should be reassessed during the audit in response to further information or risk arising.

Misstatement: A difference between a reported financial statement item and the amount, classification, presentation, or disclosure that is required for the item to be in accordance with the applicable financial reporting framework. Misstatements can arise from error or fraud.

Definition

Sampling risk arises from the possibility that the auditor's conclusion, based on a sample may be different from the conclusion reached if the entire population were subjected to the same audit procedure.

ISA 530

Non-sampling risk is the risk the auditor reaches an inappropriate opinion despite a representative sample being chosen.

Significance of the risk approach

- Inherent risk and control risk cannot be directly influenced by the auditor.
- The auditor can, however, manipulate detection risk. If they assess that inherent and control risk are high (i.e. increased risk of material misstatement) they can lower detection risk through the following means:
  - Increasing substantive testing;
  - Increasing sample sizes;
  - Using more experienced staff;
  - Increasing levels of supervision;
  - Increasing review procedures.
- By performing a more thorough audit there is less risk that the auditor fails to detect material misstatement.

Understanding the entity, its environment, the applicable financial reporting framework and its system of internal control

The auditor is required to obtain an understanding of:

- Aspects of the entity and its environment:
  - The entity's organisational structure, ownership and governance, and its business model including the extent to which the business model integrates the use of IT.
  - Industry, regulatory and other external factors.
  - The measures used, internally and externally, to assess the entity's financial performance.
- The applicable financial reporting framework, and whether the entity's accounting policies are appropriate and consistent with the applicable financial reporting framework.
- The components of the entity's system of internal control and control deficiencies.

ISA 315 (Revised 2019) Identifying and Assessing the Risks of Material Misstatement.

The auditor will use this understanding to assess the risks and design further audit procedures in response to these risks.

The information used to obtain this understanding can come from:

- The audit firm
- The audit client
- External sources e.g. internet, industry data
- The individual auditor's own experience.

Risk assessment procedures

ISA 315 requires auditors to perform the following procedures to understand the entity and its environment.

- Enquiries with management and others within the entity.
- Analytical procedures.
- Observation (e.g. of control procedures) and inspection (e.g. of key strategic documents and procedural manuals).

Analytical procedures

The basics

- Compulsory for planning and risk assessment (ISA 315).
- Can be an efficient and effective source of substantive evidence.
- Compulsory in the final review to make sure the numbers make sense (ISA 520).
- Involve calculating ratios, computing trends, proving figures in total, and making comparisons.
- May disclose anomalies; these must be investigated.
- Used to corroborate answers to enquiries.
- Involves comparisons – an individual ratio, for example, is meaningless unless compared to (e.g.) previous years, another similar company, actual v budget etc.
- When making comparisons make sure calculations use comparable numbers (e.g. numbers with similar components from one year to the next).

The main ratios

Ratio	Calculation
Gross profit margin	Gross profit / Revenue x 100
Operating profit margin	Operating profit / Revenue x 100
Inventory holding period	Inventory / Cost of sales x 365
Receivables collection period	Receivables / Revenue x 365
Payables payment period	Payables / Cost of sales x 365
Current ratio	Current assets / Current liabilities
Quick / Acid Test ratio	Current assets – inventory / Current liabilities
Gearing	Debt / Debt + Equity OR Debt / Equity
Interest cover	Profit before finance costs / finance costs
Return of capital employed	Operating profit / Equity + non-current liabilities

Exam focus

For a question on audit risk you must ensure that your answer is based on the scenario facts and not just provide a standard answer.

You must give audit risks, not business risks.

Audit risk will either be risk of material misstatement or detection risks.

Exam kit questions in this area:

Section A – Objective test case questions:

- Veryan
- Flute
- Epica
- Hawk

Section B – Constructed response questions:

- Hart
- Scarlet
- Harlem
- Peony
- Darjeeling
- Blackberry
- Prancer
- Hurling

chapter

6

Planning

In this chapter

- Benefits of planning.
- Audit strategy and the plan.
- Interim v final audit.
- Fraud and error (ISA 240).
- Laws and regulations (ISA 250).
- Quality control (ISA 220).
- Documentation.

Benefits of planning

Adequate planning helps to ensure that:

- Attention is paid to the important areas of the audit
- Potential problems are identified and resolved on a timely basis
- The audit engagement is organised and managed in order to be performed in an efficient and effective manner
- Work is properly assigned to the individual team members
- Reduces risk of giving the wrong opinion.

Audit strategy and the plan

Planning involves establishing the overall audit strategy for the engagement and developing an audit plan.

Establish overall audit strategy

- Scope:
  - engagement characteristics;
  - reporting objectives;
  - significant engagement factors;
  - preliminary activity results; and
  - the resources needed.
- Timing of when to deploy resources;
- Management, direction and supervision of resources (including meetings, debriefs, reviews etc).

Develop an audit plan

- Nature, timing and extent of risk assessment procedures.
- Nature, timing and extent of further audit procedures, including:
  - what audit procedures;
  - who should do them;
  - how much should be done; and
  - when the work should be done.
- Other necessary procedures.

Start to carry out audit procedures

The audit strategy and audit plan should be updated and revised as necessary during the course of the audit.

Interim v final audit

	Interim audit	Final audit
Timing	• Performed **before** the year-end • Early enough not to interfere with year-end procedures • Early enough to give adequate warning of specific problems • Late enough to ease the pressure on the final audit.	• Performed **after** the year-end
Purpose	Allows the auditor to spread out their procedures. Useful when there is increased detection risk due to a tight reporting deadline.	To obtain sufficient appropriate evidence in respect of the financial statements. The auditor's report will be issued once the final audit complete.

	Interim audit	Final audit
Work performed	• Documenting systems • Evaluating controls • Assessing risks that will impact final audit • Attending perpetual inventory counts • Testing of: – transactions for the year to date – material transactions, e.g. purchase of new non-current assets	• Obtaining evidence that the controls tested at the interim audit have continued to operate during the period since the interim audit took place. • Testing of: – SOFP balances – SOPL transactions – Year-end journals. • Completion activities: – Going concern – Subsequent events reviews – Overall review of the financial statements – Communication of misstatements to client.

Fraud and error (ISA 240)

RISK OF FRAUD HIGH

- Maybe reduce reliance on management representations.
- Reduce reliance on internally generated evidence.
- Increase focus on externally generated evidence.
- Reduce the materiality.
- Increase level of testing.

Definitions

Fraud: An intentional act involving the use of deception to obtain an unjust or illegal advantage.

Error: An unintentional mistake.

Professional scepticism: An attitude that includes a questioning mind, being alert to the risk of fraud, and a critical assessment of evidence.

Responsibilities

Directors

- Prevent and detect fraud and error by implementing effective internal controls

Auditors

- Obtain reasonable assurance that the financial statements are free from material misstatement, whether caused by fraud or error.
- Maintain an attitude of professional scepticism throughout the audit

Fraud risk assessment procedures

- Engagement teams should discuss the risk of fraud.
- Consider the results of controls tests and analytical procedures.
- Enquire of client how they assess, and respond to, fraud risk.
- Enquire if client is aware of actual or suspected fraud.
- Consider incentives to commit fraud e.g. performance related bonuses.

Reporting of fraud

- To management
- To those charged with governance if auditor suspects management are involved in the fraud
- To third parties if there is a duty to report
- Modify the audit opinion if the fraud is material

Laws and regulations (ISA 250)

- Obtain an understanding of the legal and regulatory framework governing the client.
- Perform procedures to identify instances of non-compliance which may affect the FS, e.g. unrecorded fines and provisions.
- Obtain written representation from management that they have informed the auditor of all instances of non compliance.
- If non-compliance is identified, report to management and those charged with governance.
- Consider whether non-compliance was deliberate and casts doubt over management integrity.

Quality Control (ISA 220)

ISA 220 Quality Control for an Audit of Financial Statements

The firm should have a system of quality control to ensure:

- Compliance with professional standards, and
- Reports issued are appropriate in the circumstances.

The engagement partner takes overall responsibility for the overall quality of the engagement including the direction, supervision and performance of the engagement.

An engagement quality control reviewer must be assigned for listed entities and high risk engagements focusing on significant matters and areas involving significant judgment.

The firm's quality control processes must be monitored to ensure they are relevant, adequate and operating effectively.

Quality control during the engagement comprises

Direction	Supervision	Review
Informing team members of: • Their responsibilities • Objectives of the work to be performed • The nature of the business • Risks.	• Tracking the progress of the audit to ensure the timetable can be met • Considering the competence of the team • Addressing significant matters arising and modifying the planned approach accordingly • Identifying matters for consultation.	Checking the audit work to ensure: • The work has been performed in accordance with professional standards • Appropriate consultations have taken place • The work performed supports the conclusions reached • The evidence obtained is sufficient and appropriate to support the auditor's report.

Documentation

Definition

Documentation means the material (working papers) prepared by, or for, or obtained and retained by, the auditor in connection with the performance of the audit. Such material may be in the form of paper or electronic media.

- The working papers must be sufficiently complete and detailed to provide an overall understanding of the audit.
- In particular, the working papers should record the auditor's reasoning on all significant matters which require the exercise of judgement, and the auditor's conclusions thereon.
- Working papers are usually split into two separate files:
  - permanent file – matters of continuing interest eg loan agreements, title deeds, systems documentation
  - current file – matters of this year's interest eg bank letter, results of audit tests.

Contents of working paper

- Reporting date
- File reference
- Name of preparer/date
- Name of reviewer/date
- Subject of working paper
- Objective
- Work performed
- Results and conclusions drawn

Benefits of documentation

- Provides evidence of the auditors basis of conclusion.
- Provides evidence the audit was planned and performed in accordance with ISAs.
- Assists with direction, supervision and review of work.
- Enables the engagement team to be accountable for its work.
- Retains a record of matters of continuing significance for future audits.

The basics

- Required:
  - as evidence of work done
  - as part of quality control, there is work to review.
- If it's not recorded it didn't take place (no evidence of the audit activity).
- If it cannot be understood, it might as well not have happened (working papers must be clear).
- Should enable an experienced auditor with no previous connection to the audit to understand the work done and conclusions reached.

Custody and retention

- They are the property of the auditor.
- Must be kept secure (implications for safe custody of paperwork and also for work kept on computers and other electronic storage media).
- Audit documentation should be retained for 5 years from completion of the audit (ISA 230).

Exam focus

Exam kit questions in this area:

Section A – Objective test case questions:

- Veryan
- Spring & Co
- Swandive

Section B – Constructed response questions:

- Hart
- Harlem
- Blackberry
- Sycamore

chapter

7

Evidence

In this chapter

- Type of audit evidence.
- Audit procedures.
- Assertions.
- Automated tools and techniques.
- Sampling.
- Relying on the work of others.

Type of audit evidence

The auditor should obtain sufficient appropriate audit evidence to be able to draw reasonable conclusions on which to base the audit opinion (ISA 500).

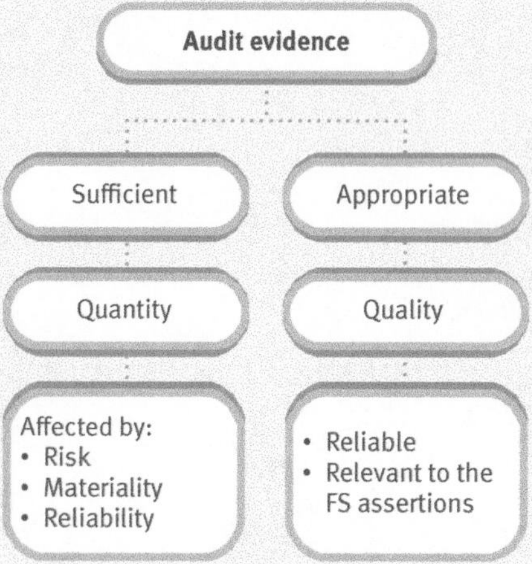

Audit evidence

- Sufficient
  - Quantity
    - Affected by:
      - Risk
      - Materiality
      - Reliability
- Appropriate
  - Quality
    - Reliable
    - Relevant to the FS assertions

Less reliable	More reliable
Obtained from inside the entity	Obtained from independent sources outside the entity
Obtained indirectly or by inference	Obtained directly by the auditor
Oral representation	Exists in documentary form
Photocopy of a document	Original document

Substantive procedures: procedures designed to detect material misstatement at an assertion level. Can be tests of detail or analytical procedures.

Tests of controls: procedures to test the operating effectiveness of the internal control system at preventing, detecting or correcting material misstatements at an assertion level.

Audit procedures

Inspection of records or documents	May give direct evidence of the existence of an asset, ownership, that a control is operating, about cut-off.
Inspection of tangible assets	Conclusive evidence of existence, may give evidence of valuation.
Observation	Involves looking at a process or procedure: may provide evidence that a control is being operated.
Enquiry	Enquiry is a major source of audit evidence but the results of enquiries usually need to be corroborated.
Confirmation	Usually consist of obtaining confirmation regarding balances or representations made by management directly from an external third party.
Recalculation	Checking the arithmetical accuracy of the client's calculations.
Reperformance	Includes re-performing management or accounting procedures, such as year-end reconciliations.
Analytical procedures	Comparisons of sets of data to identify unusual relationships or variances that could indicate fraud or error. Results of analytical reviews need to be corroborated by other forms of test.

Assertions

Management is responsible for the preparation of financial statements which give a true and fair view.

For each item in the financial statements, management are making assertions.

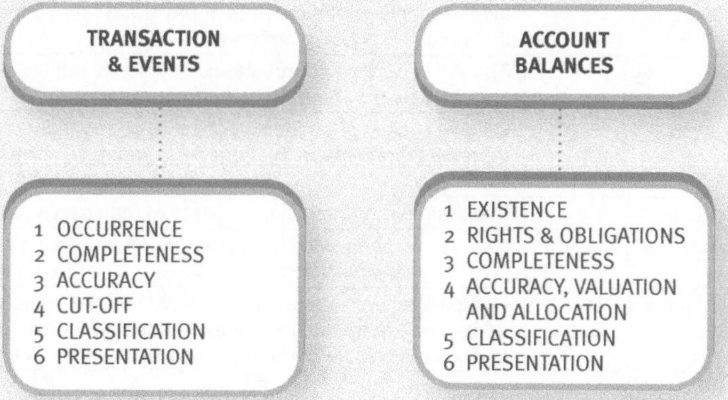

TRANSACTION & EVENTS

1 OCCURRENCE
2 COMPLETENESS
3 ACCURACY
4 CUT-OFF
5 CLASSIFICATION
6 PRESENTATION

ACCOUNT BALANCES

1 EXISTENCE
2 RIGHTS & OBLIGATIONS
3 COMPLETENESS
4 ACCURACY, VALUATION AND ALLOCATION
5 CLASSIFICATION
6 PRESENTATION

Analytical procedures as substantive procedures

- The suitability of this approach depends on:
  - the assertions being tested (maybe good for valuation, bad for existence)
  - the reliability of the data (unsuitable if controls are weak as numbers could be wrong)
  - the degree of precision possible (more suited to regular transactions than one off items)
  - the amount of variation which is acceptable (some numbers in financials require greater accuracy than others).

Automated tools and techniques

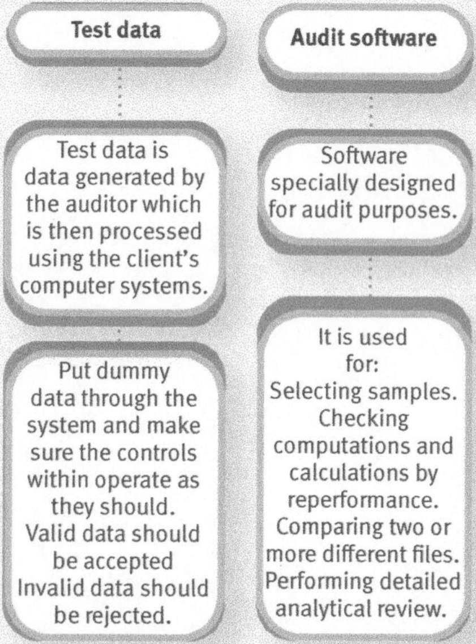

Test data

Test data is data generated by the auditor which is then processed using the client's computer systems.

Put dummy data through the system and make sure the controls within operate as they should. Valid data should be accepted Invalid data should be rejected.

Audit software

Software specially designed for audit purposes.

It is used for:
Selecting samples.
Checking computations and calculations by reperformance.
Comparing two or more different files.
Performing detailed analytical review.

Considerations affecting use

- Computer knowledge of the audit team.
- Cost/benefit analysis.
- Time available (can take a long time to set up).

Sampling

Audit sampling involves the application of audit procedures to less than 100% of the items within a class of transactions or account balance such that each has a chance of selection.

Audit sampling is usually preferable to testing all items, because:

- it would be prohibitively expensive and time-consuming to test every single item
- users of the financial statements are looking for reasonable assurance, not 100% accuracy
- full substantive testing of the accounting records will not verify that all transactions are recorded (i.e. it does not prove completeness).

However audit sampling is not appropriate if:

- population is small
- all transactions in a particular area are of great monetary significance
- population is non-homogeneous.

Designing the sample

The auditor must choose between statistical and non-statistical sampling. Statistical sampling involves random selection of a sample and then the use of probability theory to evaluate the sample results. Any other sampling approach is non-statistical sampling.

Selecting the sample

- Statistical sampling requires random selection, e.g. using random number tables or a computer program to generate random numbers.
- Non-statistical sampling requires the auditor to use judgement to select the sample items to be representative of the population.

Evaluating the sample results

The auditor carries out audit procedures on each item selected and documents the results. Errors identified in the sample are then projected across the population as a whole.

Sampling Methods:

- Random
- Haphazard
- Monetary Unit Sampling
- Systematic
- Block

Relying on the work of others

Use of auditor's experts (ISA 620)

- Auditors cannot delegate responsibility to experts.
- Examples include: surveyors, valuers, expert inventory counters, actuaries etc.
- The auditor is still responsible for obtaining sufficient and appropriate audit evidence.
- Experts must be independent, objective, competent and experienced.

Before work is performed by expert.

- Agree nature, scope and objectives.
- Agree roles and responsibilities.
- Agree nature, timing and extent of communication.
- Agree the need for the expert to observer confidentiality.

Evaluating the work of an expert

- Relevance and reasonableness of findings.
- Relevance and reasonableness of assumptions.
- Relevance, completeness and accuracy of source data.

Using the work of internal audit (ISA 610)

The external auditor may wish to rely on the work of internal audit in order to reduce the amount of detailed testing that they (the external auditor) must perform.

Assessing the internal audit function

Before any reliance is made, assess the internal audit function in terms of:

- Organisational status
- Scope of function
- Technical competence
- Due professional care.

Assessing the internal audit work

When the external auditor intends to use specific work of internal audit, they should perform audit procedures on that work to confirm its adequacy for auditing purposes.

- Sufficient appropriate evidence obtained.
- Conclusion are valid.
- Work has been properly supervised and reviewed.

Using internal audit to provide direct assistance

- Internal audit function can provide direct assistance to the external auditor under their supervision and review.
- Cannot be provided where laws and regulations prohibit such assistance.
- The competence and objectivity of the internal auditor must be considered.
- Must not do work which involves significant judgement, a high risk of material misstatement or with which the internal auditor has been involved.
- Planned work must be communicated with those charged with governance.
- Cannot make excessive use of internal auditor.
- Management must not intervene in that work.

- Internal auditors must keep the external auditor's information confidential.
- External auditor will provide direction, supervision and review of the internal auditor's work.
- External auditor should remain alert to the risk that the internal auditor is not objective or competent.

Service organisations

ISA 402 Audit Considerations Relating to an Entity Using a Service Organisation.

- Obtain an understanding of the service organisation (nature of services provided and relationship with the client, materiality of transactions) to assess the risk of material misstatement. This can be obtained through:
  - Inquiries with client
  - Confirmations from the service organisation and their auditors
  - Visits to the service organisation
  - Type 1 or Type 2 report from service organisation auditors.
- If controls are expected to operate effectively:
  - Obtain a Type 2 report
  - Perform tests of controls at the service organisation
  - Use another auditor to perform tests of controls.
- Reporting
  - Modify the auditor's opinion if sufficient appropriate evidence has not been obtained.
  - The use of the service organisation or their auditor is not mentioned in the report.

Exam focus

Exam kit questions in this area:

Section A – Objective test case questions:

- Primrose
- Hemsworth
- Spring
- Poppy
- Delphic
- Walker
- Bamboo
- Shroom
- Minnie

Section B – Constructed response questions:

- Aquamarine
- Bronze
- Lily Window Glass
- Andromeda
- Hawthorn
- Pineapple Beach Hotel

chapter

8

Systems and controls

In this chapter

- Internal control systems.
- The auditor and controls.
- Sales cycle.
- Purchase cycle.
- Payroll system.
- Cash system.
- Inventory.
- Communications on internal controls.

Internal control systems

Definition

Internal control is the process designed and effected by the directors and others to enable the achievement of the entity's objectives with regard to reliability of financial reporting, effectiveness and efficiency of operations, and compliance with applicable laws and regulations.

More reliable systems of control mean lower risk of material misstatement. Reliable systems contain stronger controls.

The auditor must: Understand the system. Understand the controls within the system. Test whether the controls work.

The more effective and reliable the system the lower the audit risk and the greater the reliance the auditor can seek to place upon the system.

More reliable system = Lower audit risk = Less substantive testing

Internal control consists of the following 5 components (ISA 315):

1 **Control environment**

- This includes the attitude and philosophy of management with regard to control e.g. a commitment to integrity and ethical values, a formal organisation structure and proper training of staff.

2 **Entity's risk assessment process**

- A more robust risk assessment process will reduce the risk of misstatement.

3 **Information system and communication**

- The auditor should obtain an understanding of the information system, including the related business processes, relevant to financial reporting.

4 **Control activities (APIPS)**

- Authorisation
- Performance reviews
- Information processing
- Physical controls
- Segregation of duties

5 **Monitoring of controls**

- Management must monitor controls to be sure that they are operating and are effective.

The 5 components can be remembered with the mnemonic **CRIME** (control activities, risk assessment process, information system relevant to FR, monitoring, environment)

IT Controls

General controls	Information processing controls
• Password protection • Back-ups • Disaster recovery • Virus checks • Restricted access • Network controls	• Batch totals • Sequence checks • Range checks • Existence checks • Authorisation • Exception reporting

The auditor and controls

- The auditor can alter the mix of tests between substantive test and tests of controls to build up the required level of assurance.
- Some substantive procedures must be carried out on all material balances.
- Remember that with tests of controls, th auditor is interested in whether controls are operating effectively – the values of the transactions are irrelevant.
- With a substantive test, the auditor is trying to gain assurance directly about a figure in the financial statements.

- The auditor needs to:

ASCERTAIN THE SYSTEM

Possible methods:

- Examine previous audit work
- Client's own documentation of the system
- Interview client staff
- Trace a transaction through the system (walkthrough test)
- Observe procedures.

DOCUMENT THE SYSTEM

Possible methods:

- Narrative notes
- Organisation chart
- Complete an Internal Control Questionnaire (ICQ or ICE)
- Flowcharts.

EVALUATE THE SYSTEM

- ICQ v ICE

ICQ

- List of possible controls
- Ask client whether the controls are in place
- Yes / No answer.

ICE

- List of control objectives
- Ask client what controls they have in place to achieve the objective.

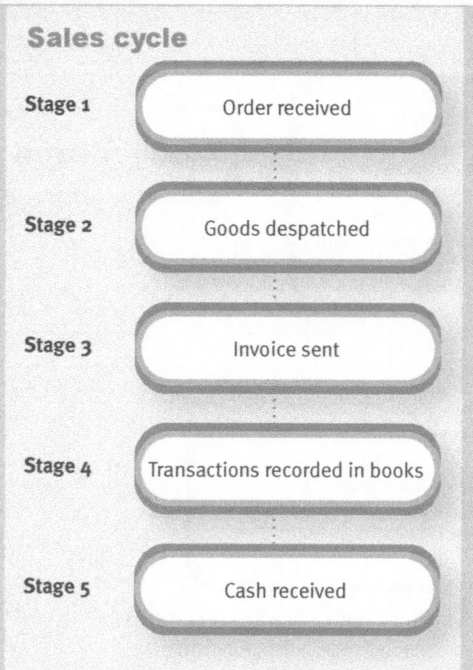

Sales system

The objectives of controls in the sales system are to ensure that:

- Goods are only supplied to customers who pay promptly and in full
- Orders are despatched promptly and in full to the correct customer
- Only valid sales are recorded
- All sales and related receivables are recorded
- Revenue is recorded in the period to which it relates
- Sales are recorded accurately and related receivables are recorded at an appropriate value.

Purchase cycle

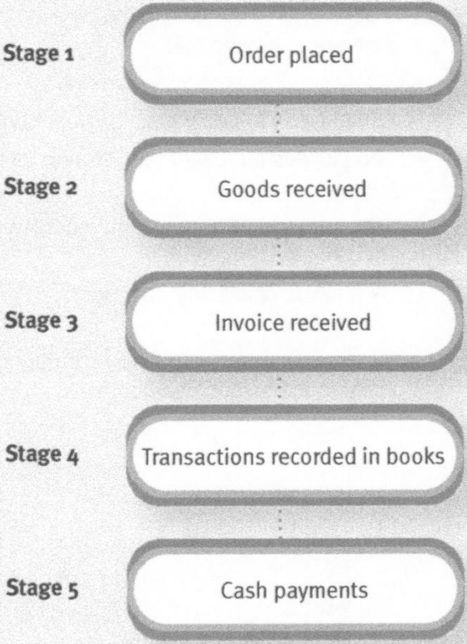

Stage 1	Order placed
Stage 2	Goods received
Stage 3	Invoice received
Stage 4	Transactions recorded in books
Stage 5	Cash payments

Purchase system

The objectives of controls in the purchase system are to ensure that:

- All purchases are of the appropriate quality and price
- Only necessary goods/services are procured
- All purchases and related payables are recorded
- Expenditure is recorded in the period to which it relates
- Expenditure is recorded accurately and related payables are recorded at an appropriate value.

Payroll system

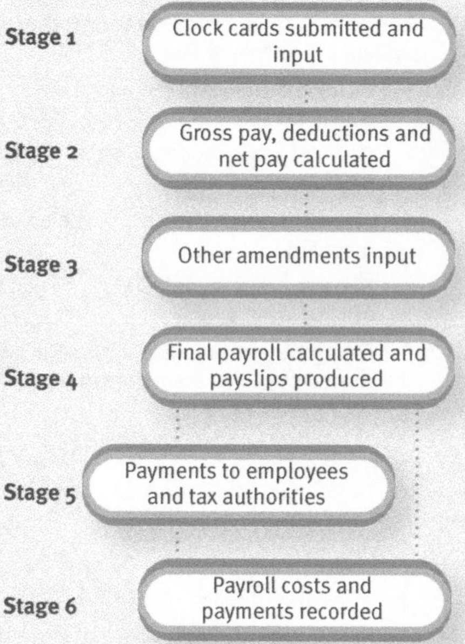

Stage 1 — Clock cards submitted and input

Stage 2 — Gross pay, deductions and net pay calculated

Stage 3 — Other amendments input

Stage 4 — Final payroll calculated and payslips produced

Stage 5 — Payments to employees and tax authorities

Stage 6 — Payroll costs and payments recorded

Payroll system

The objectives of controls in the payroll system are to ensure that:

- Only genuine employees are paid
- Employees are only paid for work done
- Employees are paid at the correct rates of pay
- Gross pay is calculated and recorded accurately
- Net pay is calculated and recorded accurately
- Correct amounts owed are recorded and paid to the taxation authorities.

Cash system

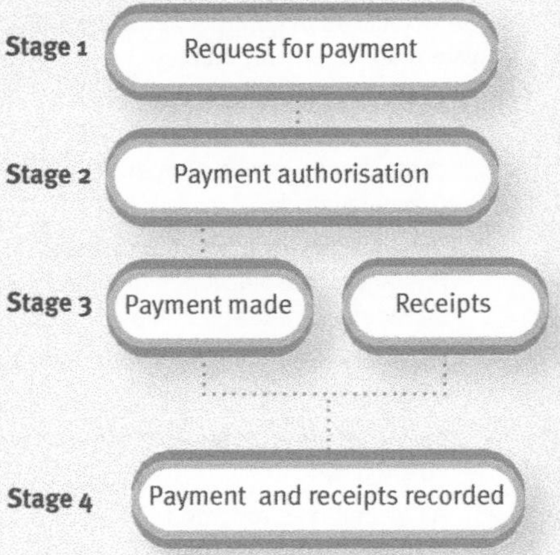

Stage 1 — Request for payment

Stage 2 — Payment authorisation

Stage 3 — Payment made | Receipts

Stage 4 — Payment and receipts recorded

Cash cycle

The objectives of controls in the cash cycle are to ensure that:

- Petty cash levels are kept to a minimum, preventing theft
- Payments can only be made for legitimate business expenditure
- Cash and chequebooks are safeguarded
- Receipts are banked on a timely basis
- Cash movements are recorded on a timely basis.

Inventory

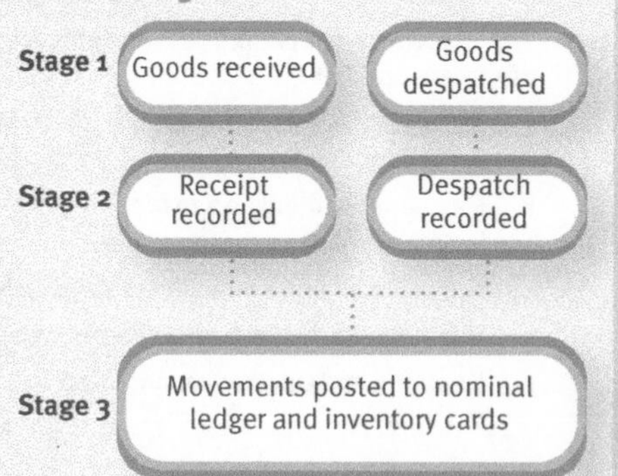

Inventory system

The objectives of controls in the inventory system are to ensure that:

- Inventory levels meet the needs of production (raw materials and components) and customer demand (finished goods)
- Inventory levels are not excessive, preventing obsolescence and unnecessary storage costs
- Inventory is safeguarded from theft, loss or damage
- Inventory movements are recorded on a timely basis
- All inventory is recorded
- Inventory is valued at lower of cost and NRV.

Communications on internal controls

The external auditor is not responsible for implementing or maintaining internal controls but needs to:

- Assess the effectiveness of internal controls.
- Communicate control deficiencies identified with management.
- Communicate significant control deficiencies identified with those charged with governance.

Communications will be by management letter or report, which is usually in two parts.

Covering letter
States that:
Only covers deficiencies identified during audit work.
For sole used of the company.
No disclosure to third parties without agreement.
No responsibility assumed to any other parties.

Appendix
Lists (often in tabular form):
Deficiencies.
Consequences.
Recommendations.
Space for management's response.

Exam focus

Questions usually focus on the content of the appendix for a given scenario rather than a covering letter.

Exam focus

Exam kit questions in this area:

Section A – Objective test case questions:

- Coastal
- Halestorm
- Primrose
- Shroom

Section B – Constructed response questions:

- Swift
- Snowdon
- Amberjack
- Freesia
- Camomile
- Raspberry
- Comet Publishing
- Equestrian
- Heraklion
- Bronze
- Trombone
- Fox Industries
- Lily Window Glass

chapter

9

Internal audit

In this chapter

- Internal audit.
- Comparison of internal and external audit.
- Outsourcing the internal audit function.
- Producing an internal audit report.

Internal audit

Definition of internal audit: an independent, objective assurance and consulting activity designed to add value and improve an organisation's operations.

The need for internal audit depends on:

- Scale, diversity and complexity of activities
- Number of employees
- Cost/benefit considerations
- The desire of senior management to have assurance and advice on risk and control.

What do internal auditors do?

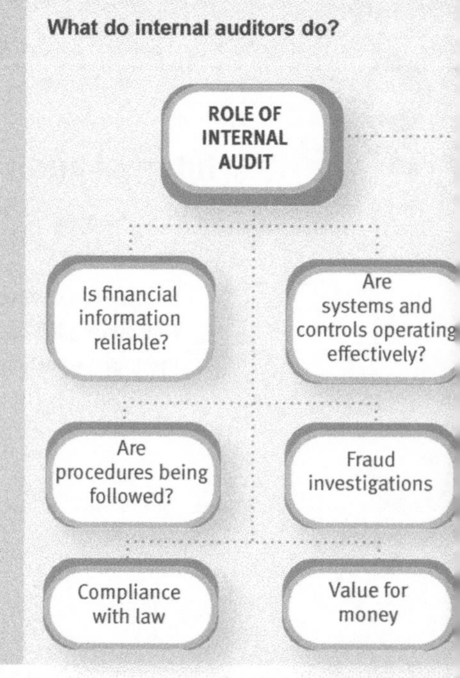

Comparison of internal and external audit

	Internal audit	External audit
Status	Employees or outsourced function	Independent
Appointed by	Audit committee	Shareholders
Reports to	Audit committee	Shareholders
Reports on	Controls, VFM, IT	True and fair view of FS
Standards	Internal audit standards	ISAs, Code of Ethics

To work the internal audit department must be:

- Sufficiently resourced
- Well organised
- Independent and objective.

Limitations of the internal audit function

The main limitations of internal audit are:

- Independence (or lack of)
- Variation of standards – relatively new profession.

Outsourcing the internal audit function

Outsourcing means finding an external service provider to perform the role, rather than sourcing and managing the role 'in house'.

Advantages

- Emphasis on cost and efficiency of the function.
- Expertise range of staff (including specialist skills).
- Staffing risks and costs passed to provider.
- May improve objectivity of function.
- Access to new audit technologies.
- Reduced management time.

Disadvantages

- Threat to objectivity if provided by external auditor.
- Potential lack of knowledge of the organisation's objectives, culture or business.
- Cost focus may reduce the effectiveness of the function.
- Service provider may not be as flexible as an in-house function.
- Lack of control over standard of service.

Internal audit assignments

The general approach

- Identify key risk areas.
- Are there any procedures to mitigate the risk?
- Are the procedures being followed?
- Are the procedures effective?
- Report and recommend.

Value for money audits

3 Es

- Economy – least cost.
- Efficiency – best use of resources.
- Effectiveness – best results.

Audit of information technology

- Do the systems provide a reliable basis for the preparation of financial statements?
- Do internal controls reduce the risk of misstatement?
- Does the system represent value for money/best value?
- Are the controls over awarding contracts for IT installations effective?

Financial internal audit

- Do the records and evidence support financial and management reporting?
- Are there errors and/or fraud?
- Does the analysis of information identify trends and potentially significant variations from the norm?

Producing an internal audit report

- Similar to report to management.
- Describe deficiencies.
- Explain the consequences to the organistion.
- Provide a recommendation for improvement.

Exam focus

Exam kit questions in this area:

Section A – Objective test case questions:

- Sistar
- Primrose
- Shroom

Section B – Constructed response questions:

- Bronze
- Raspberry
- Equestrian

chapter

10

Procedures

In this chapter

- Receivables.
- Inventory.
- Liabilities.
- Bank and cash.
- Tangible non-current assets.
- Accounting estimates.
- Statement of profit or loss.
- Smaller entities.
- Not-for-profit organisations.

Receivables

Trade receivables procedures:

- Obtain aged receivables listing, cast and agree to FS.
- Request direct confirmation from customers to confirm existence and rights.
- Inspect GDNs and invoices included in the listing to confirm amounts.
- Inspect cash received post year end to confirm valuation.
- Calculate receivables days and compare with credit terms.
- Enquire with management about any long overdue debts.
- Inspect correspondence with customers for disputes.
- Recalculate the allowance for irrecoverable debts and compare with level of old debts to assess adequacy.

Prepayments procedures:

- Inspect invoices to confirm expenditure relates to subsequent period.
- Recalculate the prepayment to verify accuracy.
- Inspect bank statement to confirm it was paid before year end.

Inventory

- Can be raw materials, work in progress and finished goods.
- Main test areas:
  - existence / completeness – attend inventory count
  - valuation.

Attendance at the inventory count

Where inventory is material the auditor should attend the inventory count unless impracticable.

Before the count

- Review the previous year's working papers for issues.
- Review the client's instructions issued to the counters for adequacy.
- Identify any problem areas and discuss them with the client.

During the count

- Observe the conduct of the count to ensure instructions being carried out properly.
- Make limited test counts to check the accuracy of the count.
- Make notes of any damaged or possibly obsolete inventory.
- Record document numbers for subsequent test of cut-off – see below.
- Reach a conclusion as to whether the count was carried out satisfactorily.
- Trace goods in the warehouse to the count sheets of completeness.
- Trace goods on the count sheets to the warehouse for existence.
- Enquire if any third party inventory is held and ensure this has been removed from the warehouse and is not included in the count.

After the count

- Inspect the inventory listing to ensure damaged/obsolete items have been written down to NRV.
- Inspect the inventory listing for the items on the last GRNs and GDNs obtained to ensure cut-off is correctly applied.
- Trace items on the count sheets obtained during the count into the inventory listing to ensure the quantities have not been changed.
- Calculate inventory days ratio and compare with prior year to identify any slow moving items requiring write down.
- Inspect the aged inventory listing for old items and discuss the need for write down with management.
- Inspect purchase invoice to verify cost.
- Inspect post year end sales invoices to verify NRV.
- Review calculations of overheads included in WIP and ensure only production related overheads are included.

Inventory stored at a third party site

- Visit third party site to verify existence of the inventory if material.
- Obtain external confirmation from the third party of the quantity and condition of the goods.
- Obtain a report from the third party's auditors confirming the reliability of the internal controls at the third party.

Standard costs

- Obtain breakdown of the standard cost calculation and agree a sample of costs to invoices.
- Enquire of management the basis for the standard costs and how often they are updated.

- Inspect the variance account and assess the level of variance for reasonableness. Discuss with management any significant variances arising.

Exam focus

You must be clear about the two separate tasks facing the auditor:

- Does the inventory exist? Attend the inventory count to find out.
- Is the inventory correctly valued?

The two tasks are inter-related, i.e. the auditor can identify damaged or dusty (slow-moving) inventory at the count, and then confirm that these inventory lines have been written down to NRV in the valuation exercise.

Liabilities

Trade payables procedures

- Obtain aged payables listing, cast and agree to FS.
- Inspect purchase invoices and GRNs included on the listing to confirm accuracy of recording.
- Obtain/perform supplier statement reconciliations to identify discrepancies.
- Obtain direct confirmation of balances from suppliers where supplier statements are not available.
- Inspect post year end bank statements for payments made which may indicate unrecorded liabilities.
- Calculate payables days ratio and compare with credit terms given to identify unusual differences and discuss with management.
- Inspect GRNs for before the year end to ensure completeness.

Accruals procedures

- Obtain the list of accruals, cast and agree to FS.
- Compare the accruals list with prior year to identify any missing accruals and discuss with management.
- Agree corporation tax accrual to tax computation.
- Agree payroll tax accrual to payroll records.
- Inspect post year end bank statements for payments of accruals to confirm the amount is reasonable.
- Inspect invoices received post year end to confirm amount of the accrual.

Loans and overdraft procedures

- Agree balances outstanding to bank confirmation letter and/or loan statement
- Inspect the loan agreement for terms an conditions such as restrictive covenants.
- Recalculate the split of current and non-current liabilities and agree to FS.
- Review FS disclosure is adequate.
- Recalculate any interest accrual to verify accuracy.
- Inspect bank statements for loan and interest payments.

Provisions and contingencies

Procedures

- Enquire with management the basis of the provision to assess reasonableness.
- Recalculate the provision to confirm arithmetical accuracy.
- Obtain written representation from management as to the adequacy and completeness of the provision.
- For a legal provision obtain confirmation from lawyers regarding amount and probability.
- Inspect board minutes to confirm an obligation exists at year end.
- Review subsequent events for further evidence.

Bank and cash

Procedures

- Obtain listing of bank and cash balances, cast and agree to FS.
- Obtain a bank confirmation letter for all bank accounts held.
- Obtain bank reconciliations for all bank accounts and cast to confirm accuracy.
- Agree the balance per the cash book to the ledger.
- Agree the balance per the bank statement to the bank letter.
- Agree unpresented cheques to the post year end bank statements to confirm they have cleared in a reasonable time.
- Agree outstanding lodgements to the paying in book and post year end bank statements.
- Perform a cash count for any material cash balances or where fraud may be suspected.

- Inspect the bank letter for any other details requiring disclosure such as security over assets.

Tangible non-current assets

Main procedures

- Select a sample of assets from the asset register and physically inspect them (existence).
- Select a sample of assets visible at the client premises and inspect the asset register to ensure they are included (completeness).
- Reperform depreciation calculations or perform a predictive analytical review calculation on depreciation figures.
- Note the condition of assets when inspecting them and relate to valuation.
- Review any valuers' reports to confirm valuation.
- Inspect title deeds, registration documents for the client's name.

Accounting estimates

An accounting estimate is an approximation of the amount of an item in the absence of a precise means of measurement.

Examples of accounting estimates.

- Depreciation charges (since the useful life and residual value of a fixed asset are only estimates).
- Provision for a loss from a court case.
- Provision to meet warranty claims.

In accordance with ISA 540 use one or a combination of the following approaches.

- Review and test the process used by management to develop the estimate.
- Use an independent estimate and compare this with management's estimate.
- Review subsequent events which provid[e] evidence about the estimate.

Statement of profit or loss

Revenue

- Compare revenue to prior year, investigate significant differences.
- Compare revenue against budget, investigate significant differences.
- Calculate GPM and compare to prior year.
- Inspect GDNs before and after year end to confirm cut-off.
- Inspect sales invoices to confirm accuracy.
- Trace GDNs into sales listing to confirm completeness.

Purchases

- Compare purchases to prior year, investigate significant differences.
- Compare purchases against budget, investigate significant differences.
- Calculate GPM and compare to prior year.
- Inspect GRNs before and after year end to confirm cut-off.
- Inspect purchase invoices to confirm accuracy.
- Trace GRNs into purchase listing to confirm completeness.

Payroll

- Compare payroll to prior year, investigate significant differences.
- Compare payroll against budget, investigate significant differences.
- Agree a sample of amounts from the payroll listing to payslips to confirm accuracy.
- Recalculate a sample of employee's pay to confirm accuracy.
- Agree a sample of names from employee contracts into payroll listing to confirm completeness.

Exam focus

This chapter includes many examples of typical procedures. When answering questions don't note down everything you can think of. Auditing requires professional judgement so always consider when answering a question:

- risks involved
- the nature of the items being tested
- assertions being tested.

Every exam contains questions requiring audit procedures.

Smaller entities

Clients that are small businesses exhibit several characteristics. They are usually:

- lower risk assignments
- under the direct control of owner managers (who know what is going on)
- have simpler systems.

But there are potential problems with:

- possibility of management override
- lack of segregation of duties.

There should be no change in the application of risk based auditing (assuming that they require, under current legislation, an audit).

Not-for-profit organisations

- Small not for profit organisations have many of the attributes of other small entities mentioned earlier.
- But such organisations tend to be staffed by volunteers.
- Their culture is more likely to be one of trust rather than accountability.
- Therefore documentation and controls may be less formal.

Audit approach

In principle, the approach should be exactly as studied so far, in accordance with auditing standards. The same ideas of audit planning, risk assessment, testing of controls, etc can be applied.

Income can be a serious problem for the auditor, since it is usually accounted for on a cash basis, with little accompanying documentation. Detailed analytical procedures and written representations from managers can assist, but the auditor may struggle to gain sufficient audit evidence of the completeness of income.

Expenditure. The NFP is likely to have certain stated aims, so expenditure must be consistent with these aims.

- Review the post year end period to compare to actual performance.
- Recalculate balances and cast.
- Review board minutes.

Exam focus

Exam kit questions in this area:

Section A – Objective test case questions:

- Chester
- Walker
- Poppy
- Eagle Heating
- Hawk
- Swandive
- Delphic
- Bamboo
- Hightown

Section B – Constructed response questions:

- Scarlet
- Sagittarii & Co
- Encore
- Spadefish
- Hyacinth
- Jasmine
- Gooseberry
- Dashing
- Airsoft
- Insects4U
- Elounda
- Andromeda
- Hawthorn
- Pineapple Beach Hotel

chapter

11

Completion and review

In this chapter

- Final review.
- Evaluation of misstatements.
- Subsequent events.
- Going concern.
- Written representations.

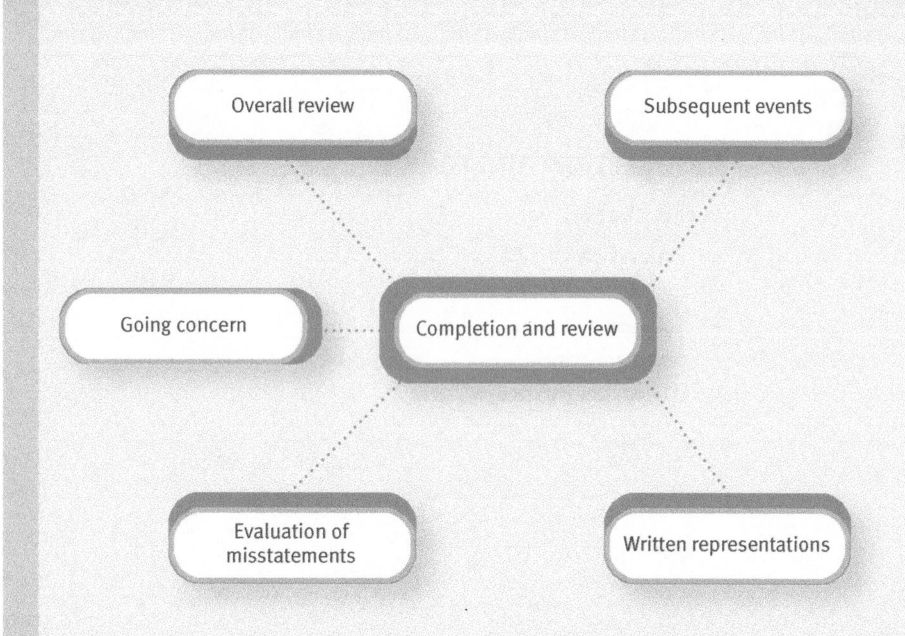
Overall review
Subsequent events
Going concern
Completion and review
Evaluation of misstatements
Written representations

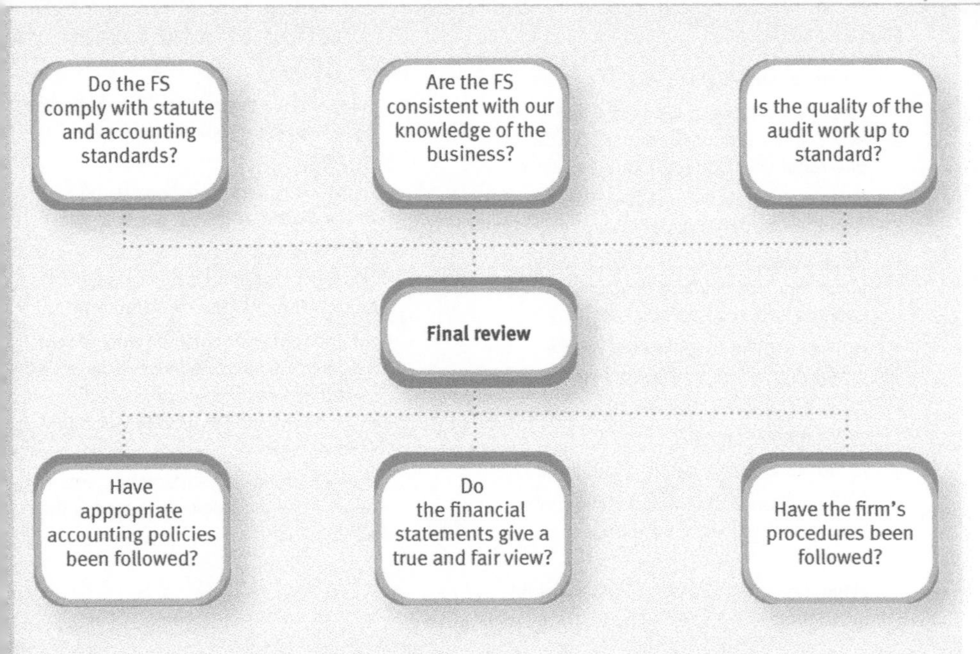
Do the FS comply with statute and accounting standards?
Are the FS consistent with our knowledge of the business?
Is the quality of the audit work up to standard?
Final review
Have appropriate accounting policies been followed?
Do the financial statements give a true and fair view?
Have the firm's procedures been followed?

Final review

The reviewer should ask:

- Has the work has been performed in accordance with professional standards and regulatory and legal requirements?
- What significant matters have been raised for further consideration?
- Have appropriate consultations taken place and the resulting conclusions been documented and implemented?
- Is there a need to revise the nature, timing and extent of the work performed?
- Does the work performed support the conclusions reached?
- Is the work appropriately documented?
- Is the evidence obtained sufficient and appropriate to support the auditor's report?
- Have the objectives of the engagement procedures have been achieved?

Evaluation of misstatements (ISA 450)

- All identified errors should be recorded on a working paper set up for the purpose.
- Individually immaterial errors may, in aggregate, amount to a material difference.
- Management should be requested to adjust all identified misstatements.
- All uncorrected misstatements should be communicated to those charged with governance and a description of the implications for the auditor's report, if appropriate.
- If any material misstatements remain unadjusted the auditor will modify the audit opinion.

Subsequent events (ISA 560)

Definition

Subsequent events are events occurring and facts discovered between the period end and the date the financial statements are authorised for issue.

Adjusting events	Non-adjusting events
Provide additional evidence about conditions existing at the statement of financial position date.	Provide evidence about conditions arising after the statement of financial position date.
Require adjustment	Require disclosure if material
• Trade receivables become irrecoverable debts • Inventory held at year-end is sold for less than cost after year-end • Estimate for a provision is revised	• Fire destroys inventory after the year-end • Injury resulting in legal action occurs after year-end • Takeover
IAS® 10 *Events After the Reporting Period*	

- Up to the date of the auditor's report, the auditor must watch out for subsequent events that might require adjustment or disclosure in the financial statements.
- The auditor is under no obligation to perform audit procedures after the auditor's report has been issued, however, if they become aware of a fact which would cause them to issue a modified opinion, they must discuss the matter with management and consider whether the financial statements require amendment.
- Procedures involve:
  - enquiry and discussion
  - review of minutes
  - review of budgets, management accounts, other financial data
  - written representation
  - normal procedures (looking at after date cash receipts, payments, cutoff etc.).

Going concern (ISA 570)

The going concern concept

Definition

A company is assumed to be a going concern if it is likely to continue trading for the foreseeable future.

- When preparing financial statements, the directors should assess whether there are significant doubts about an entity's ability to continue as a going concern.
- The auditor's responsibility is to consider the appropriateness of management's use of the going concern assumption, and whether there are adequate disclosures regarding uncertainties about the entity's ability to continue as a going concern.

Typical indicators of going concern problems

- Net current liabilities.
- Necessary borrowing facilities not agreed.
- Significant liquidity or cashflow problems.
- Substantial operating losses.
- Inability to pay debts (eg, tax payments) as they fall due.
- Loss of key management or staff.
- Loss of key suppliers or customers.

Typical audit procedures

- Review cash flow forecasts and post-year-end management accounts to analyse trends in performance.
- Review correspondence with major customers for evidence of disputes.
- Inspect correspondence from the bank to assess the likelihood of obtaining further finance.
- Inspect correspondence from lawyers regarding outcome of legal cases which could impact going concern.
- Inspect board minutes for management's plans to address going concern issues.
- Obtain written representation from management that they believe the company is a going concern.

Written representations (ISA 580)

Definition

A **Written representation** is a written statement by management provided to the auditor to confirm certain matters or to support other audit evidence.

- The auditor must consider whether the written representation letter is consistent with other forms of evidence obtained.
- The auditor must consider whether there are any concerns over the competence, integrity or ethical values of management which could affect the reliability of the written representation.
- If there are concerns over competence, integrity or ethical values the auditor should consider withdrawing from the audit.
- If the auditor cannot withdraw, a disclaimer of opinion should be given.
- Similar considerations will apply if management refuse to provide a written representation letter.

Examples of matters included in a written representation

General matters	Specific matters	Matters required by ISAs
Confirmation from management that they have fulfilled their responsibilities in relation to: • Preparing the financial statements in accordance with an applicable financial reporting framework • Providing the auditor with all relevant information and access to records • Recording all transactions and reflecting them in the financial statements	• That management believe the assumptions used for areas of judgement are reasonable • That provisions and liabilities are complete • That a particular product line is going to continue • Plans or intentions that may affect asset values	• All known and suspected frauds have been communicated to the auditor (ISA 240) • All instances of non-compliance with laws and regulations have been communicated to the auditor (ISA 250) • Management believe the effects of uncorrected misstatements are immaterial (ISA 450) • All subsequent events have been communicated to the auditor (ISA 560) • All going concern issues have been communicated to the auditor (ISA 570)

Exam focus

Exam kit questions in this area:

Section A – Objective test case questions:

- Viola Co
- Spring & Co
- Elm & Co
- Blenkin & Co
- Mississippi
- Pacific
- MMT
- Bond & Co
- Humphries
- Greenfields
- Minnie
- Panda

Section B – Constructed response questions

- Spadefish
- Hyacinth
- Jasmine
- Gooseberry
- Dashing
- Elounda
- Andromeda
- Violet & Co

chapter

12

Reporting

In this chapter

- The auditor's report.
- Elements of an auditor's report.
- Example of an auditor's report.
- Types of opinions.
- Additional communications.
- Key audit matters.
- Other information.

The auditor's report

- The auditor's report is the output of the audit.
- It contains the auditor's opinion as to whether the financial statements give a true and fair view.

Elements of an auditor's report

- Title
- Addressee
- Auditor's opinion
- Basis for opinion
- Key audit matters (if listed)
- Other information
- Responsibilities of management
- Auditor responsibilities
- Other reporting responsibilities
- Name of the engagement partner
- Signature
- Auditor's address
- Date

Example of an auditor's report

INDEPENDENT AUDITOR'S REPORT

To the Shareholders of ABC Company

Opinion

We have audited the financial statements of the ABC Company (the Company), which comprise the statement of financial position as at 31 December, 20X4, and the statement of comprehensive income, statement of changes in equity and statement of cash flows for the year then ended, and notes to the financial statements, including a summary of significant accounting policies.

In our opinion, the accompanying financial statements present fairly, in all material respects, (or give a true and fair view of) the financial position of the Company as at December 31, 20X4, and its performance and its cash flows for the year then ended in accordance with International Financial Reporting Standards.

Basis for Opinion

We conducted our audit in accordance with International Standards on Auditing (ISAs). Our responsibilities under those standards are further described in the Auditor's Responsibilities for the Audit of the Financial Statements section of our report. We are independent of the Company in accordance with the ethical requirements that are relevant to our audit of the financial statements in [jurisdiction], and we have fulfilled our other ethical responsibilities in accordance with these requirements. We believe that the audit evidence we have obtained is sufficient and appropriate to provide a basis for our opinion.

Key Audit Matters

Key audit matters are those matters that, in our professional judgment, were of most significance in our audit of the financial statements of the current period. These matters were addressed in the context of our audit of the financial statements as a whole, and in forming our opinion thereon, and we do not provide a separate opinion on these matters.

[Description of each key audit matter in accordance with ISA 701]

Other information

Management is responsible for the other information. The other information comprises the Chairman's statement, but does not include the financial statements and the auditor's report thereon.

Our opinion on the financial statements does not cover the other information and we do not express any form of assurance conclusion thereon.

In connection with our audit of the financial statements, our responsibility is to read the other information and, in doing so, consider whether the other information is materially inconsistent with the financial statements or our knowledge obtained in the audit or otherwise appears to be materially misstated. If, based on the work we have performed, we conclude that there is a material misstatement of this information, we are required to report that fact. We have nothing to report in this regard.

Responsibilities of Management and Those Charged With Governance for the Financial Statements

Management is responsible for the preparation and fair presentation of these financial statements in accordance with International Financial Reporting Standards, and for such internal control as management determines is necessary to enable the preparation of financial statements that are free from material misstatement, whether due to fraud or error.

In preparing the financial statements, management is responsible for assessing the Company's ability to continue as a going concern, disclosing as applicable, matters related to going concern and using the going concern basis of accounting unless management either intends to liquidate the Company or to cease operations, or has no realistic alternative but to do so.

Those charged with governance are responsible for overseeing the Company's financial reporting process.

Auditor's Responsibilities for the Audit of the Financial Statements

Our objectives are to obtain reasonable assurance about whether the financial statements as a whole are free from material misstatement, whether due to fraud or error, and to issue an auditor's report that includes our opinion. Reasonable assurance is a high level of assurance, but is not a guarantee that an audit conducted in accordance with ISAs will always detect a material misstatement when it exists. Misstatements can arise from fraud or error and are considered material if, individually or in the aggregate, they could reasonably be expected to influence the economic decisions of users taken on the basis of these financial statements.

As part of an audit in accordance with ISAs, we exercise professional judgment and maintain professional scepticism throughout the audit. We also:

- Identify and assess the risks of material misstatement of the financial statements, whether due to fraud or error, design and perform audit procedures responsive to those risks, and obtain audit evidence that is sufficient and appropriate to provide a basis for our opinion. The risk of not detecting a material misstatement resulting from fraud is higher than for one resulting from error, as fraud may involve collusion, forgery, intentional omissions, misrepresentations, or the override of internal control.
- Obtain an understanding of internal control relevant to the audit in order to design audit procedures that are appropriate in the circumstances, but not for the purpose of expressing an opinion on the effectiveness of the Company's internal control.
- Evaluate the appropriateness of accounting policies used and the reasonableness of accounting estimates and related disclosures made by management.
- Conclude on the appropriateness of management's use of the going concern basis of accounting and, based on the audit evidence obtained, whether a material uncertainty exists related to events or conditions that may cast significant doubt on the Company's ability to continue as a going concern. If we conclude that a material uncertainty exists, we are required to draw attention in our auditor's report to the related disclosures in the financial

statements or, if such disclosures are inadequate, to modify our opinion. Our conclusions are based on the audit evidence obtained up to the date of our auditor's report. However, future events or conditions may cause the Company to cease trading as a going concern.

- Evaluate the overall presentation, structure and content of the financial statements, including the disclosures, and whether the financial statements represent the underlying transactions and events in a manner that achieves fair presentation.

We communicate with those charged with governance regarding, among other matters, the planned scope and timing of the audit and significant findings, including any significant deficiencies in internal control that we identify during our audit.

We also provide those charged with governance with a statement that we have complied with relevant ethical requirements regarding independence, and to communicate with them all relationships and other matters that may reasonably be thought to bear on our independence, and where applicable, related safeguards.

From the matters communicated with those charged with governance, we determine those matters that were of most significance in the audit of the financial statements of the current period and are therefore the key audit matters. We describe these matters in our auditor's report unless law or regulation precludes public disclosure about the matter or when, in extremely rare circumstances, we determine that a matter should not be communicated in our report because the adverse consequences of doing so would reasonably be expected to outweigh the public interest benefits of such communication.

Report on Other Legal and Regulatory Requirements

[As required by local law, regulation or national auditing standards]

The engagement partner on the audit resulting in this independent auditor's report is ....

Signature

Address

Date

The opinion should be modified under the following circumstances:

- the financial statements are **NOT** free from material misstatement; or
- the auditor was unable to obtain sufficient appropriate evidence.

The wording of the opinion then depends upon whether the material is:

- material but not pervasive (i.e. isolated to certain elements of the financial statements); or
- material and pervasive (i.e. infiltrates so much of the financial statements that they are unreliable as a whole).

If the opinion is being modified, a 'basis for' paragraph will be included to explain the reason for the modification.

Types of Opinion

Nature of issue	Not material	Material but Not Pervasive	Material & Pervasive
Misstatement	Unmodified opinion True and fair view Basis for opinion	Qualified Opinion Except for ... Basis for qualified opinion	Adverse Opinion FS do not give a true and fair view Basis for adverse opinion
Inability to obtain sufficient appropriate audit evidence	Unmodified opinion True and fair view Basis for opinion	Qualified Opinion Except for ... Basis for qualified opinion	Disclaimer of Opinion Do not express an opinion Basis for disclaimer of opinion

Material but not pervasive – misstatements do not represent a substantial proportion of the FS

Material and pervasive – misstatements represent a substantial proportion of the FS making them unreliable as a whole

Additional communications

Material uncertainty relating to going concern

Included where the directors have made adequate disclosure of material uncertainties relating to going concern to draw the user's attention to the disclosure.

Emphasis of matter

Included to draw the user's attention to a note disclosed in the financial statements (usually in relation to fundamental uncertainties/contingencies).

Other matters

Included to draw the user's attention to other matters not related to the financial statements. e.g. further information about the auditor's responsibilities.

Key audit matters

Key audit matters are those that in the auditor's professional judgment were of most significance in the audit and are selected from matters communicated to those charged with governance.

Examples:

- Significant risks of material misstatement
- Significant areas of judgement
- Significant events or transactions

Other information

Other information is defined as financial and non-financial information included in a document containing audited financial statements and the auditor's report. Examples include a Chair's Statement and Directors' Report.

The auditor must read this information to identify any inconsistencies between the information and the financial statements or their knowledge of the client.

If the other information is received before the date of the auditor's report, a separate section should be included in the audit report under the heading 'Other Information'. In this section the auditor should:

- Identify the other information obtained prior to the date of the auditor's report.
- State that the auditor has not audited the other information and accordingly does not express an opinion or conclusion on that information.
- Include a description of the auditor's responsibilities with respect to other information.
- State either that the auditor has nothing to report, or a description of the material misstatement.

Exam focus

Exam kit questions in this area:

Section A – Objective test case questions:

- Viola Co
- Spring & Co
- Elm & Co
- Blenkin & Co
- Mississippi
- Pacific
- MMT
- Bond & Co
- Humphries
- Greenfields
- Minnie
- Panda

Section B – Constructed response questions

- Sagittarii & Co
- Encore
- Jasmine
- Gooseberry
- Dashing
- Airsoft
- Insects4U
- Andromeda
- Violet & Co

References

The Board (2020): IAS 10 *Events After the Reporting Period.* London: IFRS Foundation.

Index

A

B

C

D

E

F

I

L

M

N

O

P

Q

R

S

T

U

V

W